Whimsies & Wonderings

Poems of Everyday Life

by James Somerville

Best wishes

James Somerville

Contents

Experiences

Memories and Reflections

Senior Living

In the South

Hearth and Home

~: These homespun poems of daily life and thought have helped me navigate an often-confusing and always-complex world. Perhaps some of them will strike a cord in you and stimulate the creation of your own "whimsies and wonderings."

~: This book could never have been assembled without the creative sketches of my sister, Mary Burkhardt; the technical expertise of my brother-in-law, Al; and the loving encouragement and support of my wife, Arleen. I thank each of them profusely.

~: James Somerville is a retired member of the History Department at State University of New York at Geneseo, Geneseo, N.Y.

Experiences

Halloween's Child

Footsteps on the porchlit stairs,
And at the door
Shrill threats of "trick or treat"
By slinky cats
And Satan's imps,
Parents hovering
Half-hidden in the shadows.

The plop of candies
Into rustling bags,
As one by one the monsters
Pass in swift review;
And last

Amidst the costumed clamor
Two small brown eyes
In solemn wonderment
Upturned to mine.
Then mother's gentle plea:
"Hold out your basket, honey."

Two final plops;
The crowd departs
With shouts
To claim more sweet rewards
From other homes.

I close the door,
Return to book and easy chair,
Content; and yet
What deep pools of tenderness
Did those brown eyes
Bestir?

The Missing

Through the concourse exit doors
They flowed in a steady stream,
Toting backpacks and rolling luggage,
Clad in wrinkled jeans;
Business suits;
Hip-hugger pants;
Leather boots;
Silken blouses.
To be met, hugged,
Greeted in loud tones.
We peered intently.
She was not among them.

The stream broke into eddies
That snaked slowly towards
The down escalator
And baggage retrieval.
The last arrivals straggled in:
A tangled hairdo;
A hunched figure in a wheelchair;
A beard in denim jacket and flip-flops.
There was no sign of her.

We stood, confused.
Had she missed the plane?
An accident?
Communication failure?
No message on the cell phone.
The passenger trickle ceased;
Blue-clad airline employees emerged.
She was still absent.

Down we went
To reconnoiter the still-silent conveyor belt.
People milled in anticipation.
Family groups chatted non-stop.
A lone traveler hoisted his carry-on.
She was not to be seen.

Speculation;
Agitation;
What's happened?
What to do?
Back up the escalator.

Wait! There she is!

Disappointment

Peering into the vegetable bin
That morning,
I spied dimly
Through their cellophane bag
Three plump, red radishes
(Or so I thought),
And in my mind
Began at once to savor
Their crunchy sting
Between my teeth.

But when I crinkled back the package,
I found to my chagrin
That they were
In fact
Tomatoes.

Turtle's Fortune

A turtle crossed
The road ahead of us
As we drove to market —
A small gray shell with splayed feet,
Inching sideways right to left.
We gave it room to spare
And continued on.

When we returned
The route was clean—
No smear of shattered fragments
Bespoke a tragic ending.
Our adventurer, it seems,
Had reached the grass beyond and gone
To wherever turtles go.

Today, at least,
This patient little creature
Had enjoyed
The universe's favor.

In the College Gym

In rain or cold
We forsake the streets
And take our daily walk
In the college gym.

So round we go
At a moderate pace;

Past bleachers neatly stacked
Against the far walls,
Awaiting once more to unfold
For winter's games;

Beneath rolls of netting
Suspended on ropes
In graceful arcs
Below the ribbed ceiling;

Along intersecting lines
Of red, white, and green
That crisscross the floor,
The whites encircling
Blue rectangles that pay homage
To clear-backed hoops
Above them.

The gym is still—
Our footsteps summon no echoes—
We speak almost in whispers—

As round we go
At a moderate pace.

~: 8

Poll Watcher

I sit at a table
In the rec hall,
Opposite the other party's rep,
Crossing out names on a sheet of paper
As the voters trickle in.

There's old Mrs. Timmerman
Leaning on her cane but,
Determined to do her civic duty.
She's one of ours,
So I draw a line through her name.

And next Jake the plumber—
Wonder who's his favorite *this* year.
"Mattingly," shouts the Registrar
As Jake signs the book.
An Independent, but on my list.

Here a young woman—
Tight jeans, straight black hair—
Enters slowly and peers uneasily
About the room.
The Registrar pauses;
Consults the rolls;
Asks a question;
Then calls triumphantly,
"Abromowitz! first time voter!"
Cheers and applause across the hall.
The girl smiles fleetingly, embarrassed,
But walks decisively to the booth.
One of ours? You bet!

Next the town's leading lawyer—
The first man in a suit—strolls in,
Smiling at clients, right and left.
Not on my list.
No question how *he'll* vote.

Small knots of people gather.
A hum of conversation:
"Ed! Haven't seen you
Since the softball tourney!"
"Selma, how's your daughter?"
"Say, anyone know when
Turkey season starts?"
"You mean they moved
To the old Barnbum place?"

I catch the snatches
But my eyes are on
The columns of names before me:
Cross out;
Not one of ours;
How is that name spelled?
Which of the four Emersons is she?

It's 11 a.m.
My shift ends in an hour.
The line grows longer,
But in our little world
All is in order
As democracy pulsates
Throughout the nation.

Affirmation

Conquering the beach
In loping strides,
My throbbing heart grinning,
"Yes!"
Blood flowing joyously, freely,
Through my veins,
Pumping, pumping.
Muscles rippling.
Joints, sinews, limbs in motion;
I am fierce,
Irresistible,
All encompassing,
Confronting the years
In exuberant defiance.

Home.
On the floor stretching,
Knees to chest—
Stomach crunches 15 count.
Then roll left
And right.
Again.

Upright,
Legs, shoulders, arms, fingers
Moving easily,
Torso pivoting in tight turns.
Neck, head swinging
Left to right.
One-foot stand—adjusting—-continuing.
Lifting weights—
Straining sideways,
Upwards,
Forwards.

And rest,
Satisfaction.
Joy.
Delight.
I breathe.
I am.

Seduction

You knew your bedtime snack
Was wrong, but
The salami sandwich
Roused your taste buds
To waves of ecstasy.

Then the 10 o'clock TV movie
Ran long and violent.
You knew watching such a film
Could be dangerous,
But you enjoyed the action.

So when at last
You crawled into bed,
You were wide awake
And the bed was hostile.

The mattress—a board;
The pillow—a rock;
The sheets—scratchy;
The covers—a collection
Of anvils weighing down
Your legs and feet.

You tossed right;
You tossed left;
You pummeled the pillow;
You tossed your fist into the air;
You glared at the darkness
Surrounding you.
But gradually. . .

The mattress yielded;
The pillow softened;
The sheets turned silken;
Your covers spread caressingly
Across your body.
Your spirit drifted.
You slept.

Once more the bed
Had gentled you into slumber.
In the morning you vowed—
Once more—
That in the future
Your evening goodies
Would be healthy.
And the pictures you watched—
Tranquil.

Right.

Better, by far,
To trust in
The bed's allure.

Sheet Mystery

Striding up the hill
One summer morning,
Past empty student rooming houses,
Their occupants gone
For the season,
We suddenly encountered
An apparition:
A short sheet
Draped over a pole
Stuck in the ground
Next to the sidewalk,
And crowned with
A square of cardboard
On which was painted
Two black circle eyes
And a black mouth—
The very quintessence
Of ghostly horror.

We stopped
To speculate:
Was this the spirit
Of a departed student?
The creation of someone
Who relishes Halloween's spookiness?
A hidden message?
Or just a bit of whimsy?

We stared
And pondered,
Delighting in
The incongruity
Of the figure,
And presently
Strode on,
Chuckling.

Images

In bed I lie in silence,
Hearing only the wind's faint passing
And my own quiet breathing.
Yet beyond this space
The world still turns,
And my drowsy senses conjure up
Other nighttime settings:

A plane droning above the clouds,
Bound for bright lights and arrival's bustle;

A police car purring slowly
Through village streets;

The corner bar about to close,
Ejecting its noisy, stumbling patrons;

One rumpled student gazing dully at a computer,
A crumpled bag of chips mute witness
To his flagging efforts;

A night watchman treading the walkway
That curves around a darkened building;

A bath-robed insomniac
Staring at a TV screen showing
A flickering Garbo movie;

The jangling tumult
Of a party in an upstairs apartment.

One by one the images
Drift through my fading consciousness.
I smile.
Turn over.
Fall asleep.

Three Cacti : A Fable

Once upon a time
Three cacti
Lived together
In a small pot
Sitting on a ledge
Next to a window
That captured
The afternoon sun.

The first cactus
Rose straight and tall,
A slim, pencil figure
With ridges and needles.
It towered over
Its two companions
And basked
In the sun's rays.

The second cactus
Was short, and shaped like
A tiny ten-pin with pickers.
It grew next to
The third cactus
And was content
With its place in the pot.

The third cactus
Was smaller than
The first cactus,
But taller than the second.

It resembled
A miniature rolling pin
With white whiskers.
Because it had been positioned
Closest to the window,
The abundance of light it enjoyed
Caused it to stretch
Far out over the rim of the pot—
So far that it looked as if
It would topple
Onto the ledge
With a sudden
KERPLOP!

One day
The pot was turned
So the third cactus
Received less of
The sun's brightness.
Soon a miracle occurred:
The third cactus
Tried to regain
The solar warmth
It had lost,
And it began to straighten up.
Day by day
It stood taller and taller.
One day its tip measured
Seven inches above the ledge;
Another day the tip
Was seven and one half inches above;
A few days later
The tip had risen to eight inches above.

How straight
Would the third cactus become?
Would it eventually
Stand as erect
As the tall cactus?
No one knew.
But the third cactus,
Built like a rolling pin,
Had already revealed
A truth to be relied upon
Amidst nature's many mysteries:

Cacti love the sun.

Coco

Cheers for Coco the Corgi
As she circles the ring
At the Westminster Dog Show.

On her little stump legs,
Her short barrel body shakes,
Rippling her brindled coat,
While her tall, pointed ears
Thrust ever skyward.

Far from the Welsh country
Where her ancestors
Chased sheep across the hillsides,
She trots on,
Pink tongue protruding.

She's vying with Spaniels and labs,
And dogs with strange names,
Some bred in Australia, Belgium, or Sweden ,
Many of them champions
Of other events.
Undaunted, Coco trots on,
Giving her all.

And at the end,
When the ratings are in,
Three cheers for Coco,
Best of the herders.

The Rising

The room: grey-dark;
The clock: six a.m.
The pillow: yielding;
The covers: enveloping.

I burrow down
In the softness,
Willing time to cease
Its mindless passage.

But the minutes press on.
The clock reads 6:30.
I pull up the blankets,
Desperate to halt
The slipping moments.

My fuzzy mind pleads
For the lengthening
Of silence's emptiness,
The secession
Of the hour's creep.

Freeze the last ten minutes,
I beg,
Or the last five.
Then freeze them again.
And again.
And again.

Narrow light
Filters through the blinds.
The room assumes forms.
The alarm clamors.

Grumbling,
I rise.

Shower

Stepping into the stall
I am enveloped in spray—

Not steely, needle harshness
That assaults the pores,
Nor aimless, irregular pulsations
Leaving the body half-dry—

But a soft, soothing caress
Of my eager skin,
Like a gentle woman
Who first befriends and then
Clasps in love.

"Stay," it says,
"Be with me.
I will not fail you."

The water flows quietly.
I absorb its liquid warmth.
I stay.

Bringing in the Paper

Shuffling across
The newly-sealed driveway
In crisp early morning,
To pluck the newspaper
From its post-and-tube shelter
Atop the curb.

Sniffing the air—
Earthen smells
Of mown grass
And mulch
Mounded against trees;
A faint whiff of smoke
Hinting of fall.

Tucking the paper
Under one arm,
Back through the side door
That still needs cleaning,
Though the spider webs
Have yielded
To a heavy brooming.

Entering the house;
Unfolding the paper.
"City bets on success"
The black type cries,
Demanding attention.
Not getting it.

Climbing the stairs.
The day begins.

Making the Bed

As the day emerges,
The bed resembles
The broken ridges
Of an ancient mountain:
A crumpled wilderness
Of sheets and blankets,
With creased pillows
Askew at the head.

The work begins.
Down come the covers,
Cascading over the end
Like a silent, frozen waterfall.
The under sheet
Is pulled tight and smoothed,
And the over sheet
Spread out and made taut.

Next, each blanket, in turn,
Is tossed across the bed,
Its swells and dips flattened,
Its widths pulled equi-distant
Down the sides.

Then the pillows
Are pounded,
Plumped,
Smoothed—
Made ready to receive
Sheets and blankets,
Which are folded over
At their tops
And tucked underneath
The pillows.

A pause.
The top blanket has become
A featureless Mesa
Spreading evenly across the bed—
Truly a work of art,
But fated to disappear
Beneath the coverlet,
Which now is flung across the whole
Like a fishing net
Settling onto a tranquil sea.

More tugging ensues.
The spread's folds and dips flatten;
The pillows are submerged below
Its flowered pattern,
Their bulges
Like the rounded contours
Of well-worn hills.

A final, careful survey.
The bed is once more respectable,
Ready for the morning's greeting.

Three Brothers

Three brother elbow bones
Were torn asunder one night
By a nasty fall.
The medical people
Went into action.

The bones were re-knit
By a flexible plate and nine screws.
Then to protect the healing,
Three stout sentries
Were layered atop
The repaired break:

First, a tough bandage
Wrapped overlapping
Around the skin.
Next, a firm plastic splint
To hold the arm in place.
And last, a black sling to provide
A sturdy yet tender cradle.

Exercise and time
Will do the rest.
And the three brothers,
Once more joined,
Will face undaunted
The world's challenges.

Waiting Room

I sit amidst
Stale magazines;
A single potted plant;
The TV blaring
Quiz show questions
At furrow-browed contestants;
Old couples staring motionlessly
At the pale green walls.

Absently I page through my book,
My mind dim.
Then footsteps
As the lords of medicine
Breach my purgatory
And call me in.

The Bed

My wife sleeps in a chair,
Her left elbow bandaged,
Stiff and sore,
Victim of a streak of ice
In a frozen parking lot,

While I explore
Our bed's spacious territory,
Tumbling across sheeted space
I've not roamed alone
For over fifty years.

Like a single cowpuncher on the range,
I plunge through low-ridged flatness,
Feeling my aloneness
Even as I marvel at
The vast bedscape I encounter.

I wander side to side,
My body twisting restlessly.
Then sleep, and morning.

My wife rests upright easily,
But once her arm is whole again,
She'll reclaim her rightful place
In a region truly meant
For both of us as one.

Nantucket Hare

In her grey-bristled fur
She darts across the sandy lane
Into the dense thicket
Bordering the sandy pathway,
Becoming suddenly invisible
To the slowly encircling hawk.

She knifes skillfully
Through the entangling shrubbery,
Her body coated
With twigs and leaves,
Her whiskers twitching soundlessly,
Enclosed now in

Her shelter;
Her refuge;
Her home.

Dennison of the underbrush,
A scampering form
Who reaches her burrow
As shadows lengthen
And her babes await.

Past and Present

On our wall
Hangs a print
Of a small French village—
Simple dirt road
Running down its center;
A row of brick shops
Jutting out from the right;
A line of trees on the left
Shading the Seine River
As it winds its way north—
An appealing scene in 1884
When it was painted.
But could such a lovely view, we wondered,
Still exist
After the passage of decades?

So we flew to France to find out—
And stepped back in time.

There it stood—
The town unblemished
By modern industrial ugliness
Or mindless urban sprawl.
The street—
Paved, now, to be sure,
But still a narrow thoroughfare.
The stores—Doubtlessly rebuilt many times,
But easily recognizable.
Best of all,
The series of trees along the bank—
Still shadowing
The eternal Seine
In its slow meanderings
To Paris.

We rejoiced:
Our print rang true.
Some creations in the universe,
It seems,
Still reflect the past.

Nantucket Groove

During the year
She stares at a computer screen,
Seeking mastery of complex software;
Conducts tense performance reviews
With sensitive staff members;
Scrambles to meet
Her boss's ever-increasing demands;
Works to justify her department's policies
To dubious colleagues.

Homeward bound at six,
Bone-tired,
Weaving through dense traffic
In rain, snow, or darkness.
A hasty meal and sofa TV
Before an exhausted bedtime.

But then,
For two weeks,
There is Nantucket.

On the ferry
She watches the mainland fall away,
The boat gently rocking
Beneath white clouds,
The stern flag catching the breeze,
And she feels her neck muscles
Slowly begin to loosen.

For a time, empty water,
But soon ahead a long, low ridge
Gathered onto itself,
Filling the horizon, west to east,
And growing ever larger.

Then into the harbor,
The long-porched houses
And little cottages on stilts
Looming up past the breakwater
As the docking nears.
A quick jolt,
And soon the rumble of cars
With bicycles and storage bins
On their roofs,
Trundling down the ramp.
She and her companion
Join the line of vehicle
Inching slowly up the narrow street—
Suddenly the town engulfs her:
Fourteen days and a collage
Of experiences and impressions
To embrace.

Now her sighs come early and often.
She strolls the winding lanes
That double back on each other,
With grey colonial clapboards lining both sides,
Displaying plaques
That announce their early origins.

Eagerly she spoons thick clam chowder
In a little, outdoor café with a green awning.
That evening she savors an elegant meal
Served on a white tablecloth,
Candles gleaming,
In a busy, stone-walled grotto.

Next day
She meanders past boutiques and jewelry shops
Amidst women in fashionable sundresses
And men in khaki Bermudas,
While local vegetables sell from wooden crates
On the cobblestoned main street.

Beyond the town,
She scans heather-covered hills
Dotted with clumps of pine,
And glimpses sprawling family homes
Perched on cliffs overlooking the sea.
She hikes sandy trails leading to the ocean,
Where blue-green waters lap the shore
And gulls wheel
Under an azure sky.

On her time share deck,
She relishes the tartness
Of a second gin and tonic
While her gaze fastens
On a little pond half-hidden
In the bushes behind the house

Day by day,
She feels the fragments of herself
Regaining the wholeness they had lost.
Her jaws relax;
Her back straightens;
Her arms swing exuberantly.
Enriched by the island's pleasures,
Her spirit soars,
She finds peace.
And joy.

But soon enough
Time's reprieve expires.
As she climbs aboard the ferry
Under a graying sky,
Tears slip down her cheeks.
And yet her eyes
Still gleam.

Paris Smiles

They were twenty somethings
Sitting at a sidewalk café
In the heart of Paris.
He ordered champagne
With a flourish.
Does this mean. . ., she thought.
Suddenly a small box
Appeared on the table
And he was slipping
A ring on her finger.
He smiled shyly at her.
Her eyes glistened.
She smiled broadly at him.

And the city
Smiled at them both.

Juxstaposition

Yesterday my wife and I
Consulted our financial advisor
In the city.

Our route wound through
Low hills dotted with:
Weathered barns
And crawling tractors;
Grazing horses,
Still in their blankets;
Thin clumps of trees
Alternating with cattle farms;
Well-built brick houses
Perched atop sloping green lawns;
One small town
Still showing vestiges
Of its historic quantness.

The city's outskirts loomed.
We reached our destination—
A blandly modern professional building—
And entered a suite of offices
That bespoke money:
Dark walnut paneling;
File drawers built into the wall;
Doors that closed noiselessly;
A small table filled with
Current financial journals.

Our casually-dressed advisor
Greeted us.
We convened around
A conference table richly brown
And finely textured,
And took seats in softly cushioned chairs.

We discussed:
Investment strategies;
The value of
Various mutual funds;
Five-year interest rates;
Tax liabilities;
And other monetary abstractions.

We concluded our business;
Small talked a bit;
Shook hands;
And returned,
With relief,
To a world of earth and sky.

Squirrel's Quest

The day was hot.
Nothing stirred.
The leaves drooped wearily.
I crouched in the shade, resting,
My breath coming slowly,
My tail limp.

He rose suddenly
From the bench
On which he'd been lounging.
He reached into a wrinkled paper bag,
Pulled out four soft-shelled peanuts,
And scattered them
On the grass.

He looked at me
And tossed out several more.
I watched carefully,
Quivering slightly,
Then hopped forward cautiously.
I seized a nut in my paw
And sat up.
My teeth scissored rapidly
As I munched.

He smiled.
I raised a paw,
Chattering shrilly.
He crumpled the bag in his hand,
Nodded to me,
And strode down the path.

I watched him go.
Then, grasping two more nuts
Between my teeth,
And flicking my tail happily,
I scampered up my tree.

Memories & Reflections

Comforts

Before my shades are drawn,
I recall sure comforts
In all my ages,
Each a distinct fragment
Of others
Lost to memory.

To wit:

In childhood,
Mother's caresses
While astride her lap;
Steering my toy truck
Across a purple rug.

Those of grade school years:
Roller skating down the sidewalk;
The luxuriant ease
Of summertime gym shoes.

Next, adolescence:
A soft bed;
A sturdy home;
A thick book that fascinates.

During young manhood:
A coed's smile
In answer to
A shy flirtation;
An "A" grade
On a lengthy paper.

Then the all-encompassing career:
Having a job;
Having a job I like:
Having a job
I'm reasonably good at.

On to senior moments:
Lolling in my easy chair,
Glass of wine in hand,
Loving wife beside me.

These and many other comforts
Have blessed my passing stages
And provided rejoinders
To life's continuing uncertainties.

Mayfly Memories

In the summer dusk
The mayflies came,
Swarming up by the thousands
From the bogs and lowlands
Of Green Bay,
The narrow finger of water
Just north of town.

We boys collected
Their thick, wriggling bodies
In mason jars and chased
The screaming girls,
While our mothers clucked vainly
For us to desist.

Their oily forms littered the streets
And thickened windshields,
Causing cars to swerve and jackknife,
While evening walkers
Crunched their feathery wings
And risked a fall.

In the ballpark ,
Where our D League Bluejays played,
A dark, pulsating mass
Had covered the centerfield light
By the time we stretched
In the seventh inning.

We heard faint tinklings
As the insects' weight
Shattered the glass.
Triumphant, our Green Bay flies
Assaulted a second light,
And sometimes a third.
The game grew dim.

What would summer have lacked
Without these legions
Of nightly visitors,
Whose mindless sacrifices
Provide the stuff
Of memories?

Grandpa's Dutch

My mother's father
Came from Holland in his early 20's
Because he wanted to be a farmer
And his family grew only tulips.

He worked the Dakota wheat fields.
Married my grandmother.
Bought land in northern Wisconsin.
Raised chickens, sheep, and cows.
Planted corn and raspberry bushes.
Sired four children.
Learned English.
Became a citizen.

At breakfast each day,
Before he ate his porridge,
He would mumble a few words.
When I visited the farm as a boy,
I sat at his right hand and strained to hear
Just what the old man was saying.
I never could.
What horrible diction,
I thought disgustedly,
And why does he swallow his words like that?
But perhaps I need to listen even closer.

Only years later did I learn the Truth:
My grandfather's way of preserving
Memories of the Old Country,
Was to recite his prayers
In Dutch.

Governance

In the vast realms of space
Throb black holes,
Their gravitational pull so fierce
That no light can emerge.

Not to be outdone,
We earthlings
(Especially Americans)
Create our own black holes,
Whose myriad gaseous elements
Are so endlessly locked
In deadly embrace
That no illumination or intelligence
Can ever escape.

These are known
As legislatures.

Big Bang God?

Picture space:
A tiny cube—
Smaller than a sugar cube—
Very hot and dense,
Floating around
In a smooth, timeless soup.

This was all there was
Before the Big Bang.

Now imagine,
Something called Cosmic Inflation
Comes along
(Just in the neighborhood, I guess),
Bursting with energy,
And in a trillion, trillion, trillionth of a second
(Who's counting?),
Explodes that teeny cube
With a huge bang—
Kaboom!
And releases particles called quarks,
Which fly out
Every which way
And turn into protons and neutrons
(Don't ask me how).

Clocks start.
Times begins.
Our universe
Is open for business.

So that's how it all began,
Give or take
A few details.
They say this Cosmic Inflation
Was just a random thing—
Could have happened anytime,
Given the right conditions.

Still, I wonder:
Might there have been
A mind of some kind,
Far beyond yours or mine,
Shaping, directing,
Pulling levers and such,
Saying at one point,
"Go for it, Cosmic Inflation!
This is the right time
To create a universe!"

I don't know.
Most likely the scientists are right:
There's no mind up there—
At least, none I could have a beer with.

But I'd sure like
To find out.

Whirlwind

Our mixing bowl universe
Tumbles, churns, swells;
Blends, melds, separates;
And mingles again
Without pattern, purpose, or meaning,
A kaleidoscope rotating endlessly
In a dance eternal.

In a crowded restaurant
People sit slurping coffee
And crumbling bread;

Next door to the beat
Of a clamorous rock concert.

In a hospital bed
A woman writhes in pain.

Down the street, computers clatter
In a cavernous, neon-soaked office.

Somewhere a politician declaims non-stop
In a near-empty chamber.

Countryside, a plow
Turns over the brown earth.

At a library table
A student peers
At a chemistry textbook.

Across the sea
A savage battle erupts
In a war-ravaged village.

Still,
Gentle ocean waves
Lap across toes
At a midnight rendezvous,
And the hard sun seers
A long line of trucks and carts
Snaking down a pot-holed, gravel road.

Each scene melts
Into life's ceaseless jumble;
Yet each creates
Its own instant mini-world,
And we stumble,
Moment to moment,
As fate decrees,
From our fragile atom being
To the whirlwind
Surrounding us.
And back again.

Permanence

You can count
On the tall conifer—
Until it topples
In a windstorm.
Likewise, the stream
Glides eternally—
Save when it dries up
Under August's sun.
And certainly the anchor
Holds the sailboat steady—
Unless the waves part
Its rotted line.
But then, the meadow
Will ripple tomorrow—
Except when buried
Under a pounding four-lane.

Drowning,
We grope for sea rocks
Too slippery to grasp,
Or murmur to ocean Gods
And taste salt in our mouths
In reply.

And should we, by chance,
Find the shore,
Is what lies ahead
But broken trees,
Parched brooks,
Severed lines,
And savaged meadows?

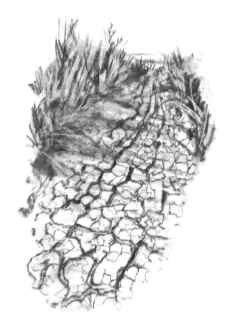

The riddle prevails:
What braces life's kaleidoscope
Against the jumble of days?
Is there sect or belief—
Idea, ism, or paradigm –
That cuts to the truth each time,
Singing clear
In the blistering sun
And when the rains fall?

Or are we fated
To ride the carousel endlessly,
Clasping each other in pathos—
And hope, yes, always in hope—
As we whirl,
And discovering
When we at last slip off,
That the falling's
The only refuge?

Unknowns

Does a field of grass
Equal a galaxy of stars?
Can a bed of black-eyed susans
Compete with Jupiter?
And should tomato plants
Confront the rising moon?

Such enigmas,
And more:
How shall we grasp
Earth's random couplings—
Grasshoppers pivoting
To embrace the sun's deep warmth;
Grey geese flapping
Toward a mountain height;
One speck of dust
Contesting fire's domination?

Do the ancient puzzles
Still ring through time,
Or are the final formulas
Being written
In this year's test tube runs?
Shall we unlock perplexity
With a computer key,
And so program the shrinking universe
To our smirking satisfaction?

Or do we,
In truth,
Uncover,
Reveal,
Set forth,
Delineate ad infinitum—
To find that yet more mysteries
Defy our smug assumptions?

Mission

Forget your complex theories
And indisputable laws;
The universe boils down to this:
A struggle between light and dark.

So let there be light
Shrinking the early morning shadows;

Pooling on a sidewalk
Unimpeded at midday;

Streaking against a corner wall
In early afternoon;

Dappling 'neath an overhanging elm
As day wanes;

Bathing a parlor chair
Encompassed within evening's blackness;

Casting wavery forms
In a candled room;

Beaming narrowly down a pathway
Obscured by nightfall;

And ever
Piercing through time's lurking gloom
In resolute defiance of despair.

Science

Give me a fact
Dug from the earth;
Gleaned from the stars;
Chiseled from bones;
Extracted from chemicals.

Give me a fact,
Cold, hard, unforgiving,
To anchor reality
When all else is blue haze
That drifts away and is lost.

Give me a fact
Rigorously analyzed,
Constantly replicated,
Endlessly debated,
Frequently modified,
And sometimes refuted,
To be replace by
A deeper fact,
A new anchor,
The world's truths
Revealed further
By an inch or a mile.

Give me a single, gleaming fact
To stand upon when all else
Is speculation;
Obfuscation;
Distortion;
Hypocrisy;
A weightless fog
That beclouds and misleads.

Others may take refuge
In elaborate chimeras
Or rigid formulas.
I'll stand on facts.

Monologue

You want meaning?
I will give you meaning.

The earth is flat
And the moon is round;
The desert sun is hot
And winds blow across the waters;
flowers grow on grassy hillsides
and creatures roam land and sea;
Men make love,
Worship Gods,
Fight wars,
And do brave and terrible things.

This is all the meaning there is.
Now be happy.

Moderate Path

I'm not climbing any more mountains
(Not that I ever did),
Or swimming in any more seas
(Never a common pastime),
Nor battling a wild, raging lion
(something I've managed to avoid),
Nor even running two miles a day
(Now *that* was a regular thing).

Spare me the strenuous life
In favor of a walk in the park;
I'll eschew those great, rippling muscles
If I can just stay flexibly fit.

For what's the sense of a cramp,
Or a ligament painfully bent,
When keeping the belly in shape
Is a laudable goal in itself?

So
I'll watch what I eat and how much;
Hold the wine to one glass a day;
Keep the exercise light,
Think virtuous thoughts,
And tread the moderate path.

Academic

My years have bred singularities—
A topography of narrow circles
Defines my days and nights.
My knowledge is precise, particular,
Divorced equally
From barbecues and carpentry,
Car repairs and fishing trips.

I gap in puzzlement
At clothing styles,
Playing cards,
And high finance,
While a computer's wiles
Hurls me, flaylingly,
Into lonely cyberspace.

I'm one-dimensional
To the bone
(Don't ask me about ocean tides
Or raising pups).
A knitted brow being
Who yet enjoys
Wine and football,
Sun and warmth,
And passion's intense embrace.
And somehow doggedly
Navigates the lurking shoals
Of each passing hour.

Defiance

Noiselessly
We slip past
The galaxies' cold glitter,
To anchor ourselves
In earth's trees, grass,
And contoured hills.

We turn from barren stars
To play out our sadness and joy
'Midst air and water,
Fertile soil,
Warmth and cold,
And our myriad kindred selves.

Space shall evolve, expand, prevail;
We shall not heed,
For ours is yet a small reality
Of birds and beasts
And human arts,
Of earth-enraptured creatures
Whose dwelling place is but a speck
In time's pitiless eternity.

Still—fiercely—no matter.
Our home abides for our days.

To hell with vastness.

Earth-Bound

I'll walk the narrow streets
Beneath sheltering elms
And dappled sunlight,
Admiring summer's lusty grass
And the season's radiant flowers.

I'll ignore
The cold vacuum of space:
Star clusters wheeling
Across enormities of vastness,
Colliding , exploding into giant plumes.
The sun destined
To vaporize earth
In seven billion years.

What are such cataclysms to me?
I measure time in inches,
One day an eternity.
The fate of a million stars
Caught by a telescope
Matters less to me
Than the atoms in my little finger
Or the growling of my stomach.
Nor do trenches on Mars—-
Deeper, more awesome
Than America's Grand Canyon—
Match the beauty
Of black-eyed susans
In my own backyard.

So in books I will read
Of the universe's features;
Study its immensities;
Ponder its future.
But until I return to nothingness,
Each moment and particle of my being
Belongs to this tiny grain of planet
Streaking through the heavens.

Little Things

I cherish little things
'Midst life's unfolding years:

Green shoots
Peering from the soil;

Small dogs
Curled up on friendly laps;

Bright goldfish
Darting in a bowl;

Pink babies
Gurgling merrily;

One teddy bear
With glossy fur;

A child's rocker
Painted red.

For what is the sense
Of earth and sun
Without the joys
Of little things?

Essences

I speak of the essence of things:
One corn kernel
Reposing on a plate;
A pea
Peering from a half-slit pod;
A single paw print
Impressed upon a muddy trail;
A broken shingle
Dangling from an empty house;
Two tattered chairs
Pitched awkwardly against a tree;
This poor planet
Spinning across an infinity of stars.

I speak, as well, in riddles:
Meaning lies in the core;
And the core defines each person,
Who needs shape his own essences
Amid life's confused cacophony.

The Vow

I'll embrace
My little slice of life:
Colored leaves of every hue;
Letters on a flowing page;
An ice cream sundae's cool delight;
My wife's quick, loving smile;
And more.

But when earth's contours fade
And I approach nothingness,
Before I cross that line
I will,
I vow,
Leave behind one subtle quip
To be remembered by.

God of Hope

I pray
Not to the God
Of Abraham or Isaac,
Nor the Jesus-God
Of Christian lore,

But to the God of hope,
The little bird in the blood
Who trills amidst
The mindless blur of days;

The thin garden reed
That defies the winds
Under a November sky;

One streak of golden sun
That, undaunted,
Pierces each blackening cloud.

My prayers fall unheeded
On theology's stony babble
And ritual's empty murmur,

But hope—my God imperishable—
Survives the quick sands
Of unfolding years,

And silently weighs
Each random plea.

Senior Living

Circles

Now he is 79.
He studies cosmology;
Reads about
America's barbarous years;
Writes dense little poems;
Finds new charms
In his loving wife;
Walks village streets
Forty minutes each morning;
Eats baked fish and vegetables
Once a week;
Sets out the trash on Fridays;
Prays every night—
To whom or what
He does not know.

Sometimes in senior moments
He wonders if these varied rhythms
Describe some vital purpose
Beyond his ken;
But then he remembers
His hard-won truth:
Meaning resides
In each event
As it happens,
And nowhere else.

Thus the circles close.

Contrasts

Immersed in books these days,
I explore cosmology's spaces
And history's determinants,
Even as simpler moments
Seek entrance to my realm:
Weeding the garden;
A short trip to market;
Eating one juicy apple;
Bantering with my wife.

Accompanying my abstract ponderings
On how the universe evolved,
Is the morning walk;
My ongoing quest for meaning
Shades into an afternoon nap;
Along with musings on religion
I gaze at the trees surrounding our house.

Profound or trivial,
Each activity carves out
Its own reality,
Yet all meld together
To create the wholeness
That I seek.

Interval

Between the working years
And the body's humbling;
Before the icing over of the brain,
There comes a time
For pondering ageless questions
And celebrating personal pleasures:

The tragedies of humankind
And walks along the seashore;
Fate's inexorable decisions
And laughter with friends;
The universe's mysteries
And wine's boundless joys.

Then when the bones
Commence to ache,
And a blue haze
Engulfs the mind,
We shall recall,
However dimly,
The quiet blessedness
Of those hours.

Achievements

Retired,
I sit in the sunshine
Reading my magazines,
While outside
The universe unfolds.

I learn
Of a dictator's rise and fall;
About the lasting genius
Of Ernest Hemingway;
How to access a horse's lameness—
Small fragments of truth extracted
From earth's rich kaleidoscope.

Then at Happy Hour
I impress my wife
With my daily quotient
Of knowledge gained.

Don't laugh;
There's much satisfaction
To be had
In small achievements.

Snoozing Process

The novel enthralls
As the plot unfolds.
But after two pages
My eyelids sag.
I blink disgustedly.
The words blur.
I blink again.
The print wavers.
Slowly my eyes close.

Under their lids
My mind roams
Down varied pathways:
Who I spoke to yesterday;
The nature of the universe;
My next Friday's activities;
Autumn's colors.

Abruptly my eyes snap open.
I read.
The plot thickens,
But my lids slip downward again.
I slump in my chair.

Outside, the world still revolves:
Semi-trailers pound endlessly
Over the freeway;
Politicos argue fiercely
In chambers;
Papers get shuffled
On elegant desks;
The sun follows its course
Across the sky.

But me?
I snooze in my easy.

~: 81

Morning Rise

Nothing describes senior hood
More vividly than the morning rise.
The sleep-glutted body protests;
The lower back throbs;
Legs wobble;
Bowels rumble ominously;
The hair stands spike erect;
The eyes without specs
Refuse to focus;
Shoulders hunch.

But a short shuffle to the bathroom;
Splashings on the face;
Rump on the toilet;
Quick comb pass;
Glasses on the nose;
And resurrection begins
As breakfast and full wakefulness loom.

The Reminder

One may commonly observe:
A luscious cherry
Atop an ice cream sundae;
One modest little button
Hugging a graduation hat;
Gawky pigeons
Teetering on a slanted roof;
A silver cross
Completing a church spire
(denomination, your choice).

But a vial of pills
Crowning a wine bottle?
Yet there it sits,
Filled with 90 capsules
Of medical miracles,
Confidently astride
The protruding cork
Of a half-empty cabernet sauvignon,
A mute reminder to my wife
To take a pill each day
Before Happy Hour.

Haughty, expectant, starkly visible,
It brooks no contradictions or exceptions,
Blocking the way to vino bliss
Until its object is fulfilled.

What next?
A pill box in a shoe,
Or hidden in the underwear?
Perhaps embedded in a cottage cheese carton
Or taped to the TV screen?
All likely hostages
To our faltering memories.

Oh, well—
Whatever works.

Removal

They were a tight crowd—
One hundred-odd history journals
Packed together on three shelves
In his study,
Covering the whys and wherefores
Of early American history;
Read religiously by him
As each issue arrived,
And consulted thereafter
Whenever his knowledge
Of the field lagged.

Then he retired.
The journals sat unused,
Gathering dust and taking up space
As newer readings accumulated
In make-shift shelving.

But the journals
Had been his lifeblood for so long,
With scribblings in the margins
And long passages underlined.
He couldn't bear to discard them.

Years passed.
More new books piled up,
Each needing a decent space
In which to be displayed.
Then one day he stood before the journals,
Gulped once or twice and,
Lifting them from
Their time-honored homes,

Carried them in his arms
To waiting trash bags.

The deed was done.
The shelves gapped empty,
Needing only to be cleaned
Before receiving their new occupants.

His life moved on.

Senior Gluttony

With the gold watch
Disappear work routines
And orderly days
As time's vacancies lay a curse,
And infirmities mount.

Now the groaning table becomes
Truly his oyster.
No more careful refusals
Of a second piece of pie;
The beast is unleashed.
In his dotage his eyes behold,
With unblinking pleasure,
Food's endless enticements.

His head throbs—
He devours a heap of mashed potatoes,
And sausages sizzling with onions.

Nothing cures an aching back
Better than a hamburger
Overflowing with melted cheese,
Tomato, bacon, lettuce, what- all.

When his mind blanks out—
All too common these days—
A deeply crusted pizza
Assuages the frustration.

Do his gums ache and bleed?
He summons sweet tooth power
With three-layer cakes;
Ice cream drowned in chocolate;
Thick milkshakes.

His waning eyesight
Still focuses lovingly
On a rich cheesecake
Drenched in cherry sauce.

The broken world he inhabits
Becomes jollier
With a stein of beer
Or scotch on the rocks
(hold the rocks).

So he eats and drinks greedily,
Grows heavier,
Moves sluggishly,
Ignores his doctor's warnings.

Such ecstasies to be had
In the tasting, chewing, smacking—
Juicy repasts stretching until
Eternity beckons.

And then—who knows—
Perhaps heaven is really
An all-you-can-eat buffet.

Valentine Party

At dusk
They left their condos
And headed for the rec center
Bearing gifts,
Carefully depositing each item
On a large table:

A tasty array
Of platters, trays, bowls, and pans
Filled with
Colorful salads, fruits, and vegetables;
Steaming corn casseroles;
Mixtures of baked, green and lima beans;
Creamy cold slaw;
Jell-O molds.
On a short stand nearby
Rested a succulent ham loaf
And two inviting chocolate cakes.

Scattered across each of the long tables
That ranged the room
Were small paper hearts;
Shiny colored beads;
Bouquets of flowers;
And small plastic champagne glasses.

As more people arrived,
The room exploded
Into conversation,
Laughter,
Hugs,
Back slapping—
A seething mélange
Of voices and bodies.

All of them were in the senior years,
Yet still vigorous;
Forgotten for now
Were the broken bones;
Aching muscles;
Heart murmurs;
Stomach ailments;
And hospital stays
Of advanced age.

Each found a seat;
The champagne flowed;
The feast began
In orderly fashion,
Table by table.
Lines at the food table,
Everyone digging in
With unconcealed relish.

After the repast,
A raffle—
Two tickets for a dollar;
Six tickets for five.
The winnings:
Restaurant certificates
And bottles of wine.

Lastly, a dance,
Complete with DJ and strobe lights,
The music fast and slow.
The dancers swaying
With relaxed smiles.
They had faced life's challenges—
Sick children;
Work stress;
Aging parents;
Money shortfalls;
Health issues;
Retirement uncertainties—
And come through intact.

Now they danced
In exuberant release
And for the pure joy
Of being
At the Valentine party.

Water Aerobics

In their flowered bathing suits,
Twelve ladies of mature years
Line two sides
Of the courtyard swimming pool,
Awaiting orders from the CD player
On the grassy slopes above,
Their laughter rippling
Across the placid waters
In which they bob.

"Leg circles," the CD booms,
And twelve pairs of arms
Grasp the sides of the pool
So that twelve pairs of legs
Can obediently rotate
First above, then below the surface.

"Now turn and Kick," the CD directs,
And twelve bodies flip over,
Regain their grips
On the pool's tile rim,
And commence a noisy splashing.

More directions follow:
Scissors movements;
Legs elevated, out of the water;
More splashing—
The ladies are in
Continuous motion.

Next, a series of arm movements.
Obeying the CD,
The ladies form a circle,
Flailing their arms
Just below
And just above
The water.
The CD's rapid instructions
Mingle with
The ladies' giggles and chatter,
Their faces a mixture
Of earnestness and pleasure.

When the lesson is over,
Some of the ladies,
Treading water,
Remain to schmooze,
While others clamor out,
Towel off,
And go on their way,
Each secure again
In the knowledge
That whatever their ages,
Weaknesses,
And afflictions,
They had once more
Mastered the waters.

In the South

Season's Dissent

I'm tired
Of poets rhapsodizing
Pretty falling snow
Blanketing the hills
And mantling the trees;
Icicles dangling gracefully from eves;
Clear nights displaying
Their cascade of stars;
Brisk breezes swirling
Round snug farmhouses
With fires in their grates so cozy.

Rubbish!

What's romantic
About reddened ears,
Stiffened fingers,
Benumbed toes,
Snot that freezes in the nostrils,
Wind that curdles the insides,
Cold that paralyzes the throat,
Four walls that become a prison cell
Through long winter months.

No,
Florida's the place
When February's mercury plunges.
Keep your watering eyes
And hacking cough,
I'll take
The sun;
The beach;

Blue sky;
Enveloping warmth.

The warmth.
Above all, the warmth.

From the Condo Deck

In the surf
The eternal fishermen
Standing straight,
Their poles firmly planted,
Waiting for the lines to jerk.

Behind them,
Slow walkers in the sand
In ones and twos,
Refugees from winter blasts.

In the courtyard
Pool water glistens.
Couples leisurely
Clink shuffleboard discs.
Above,
Gulls glide the gentle winds,
White forms
Against a cloudless blue.

This is a moment,
Rare enough,
That requires savoring,
Soon to be tucked away
To remember in harder times.

Stability

The stock market plunges
And recovers in its endless cycle.
Faster computers
Accelerate data output.
Men fight and die forever
In desert lands.
Rain forests retreat
Mile by mile.
The world roils and churns,
Its kaleidoscope
Forming, then dissolving, endless patterns.

But this year
Gulls still waddle stolidly
Across the sand;
Egrets search daintily for fish
In the gentle surf;
The big-mouthed pelicans
Glide quietly over condo roofs;
The ocean greets the shore
As it has for untold years.

In small things
Constancy carves out its niche,
A balm for harried minds
And aching bodies
Daily oppressed by the drumbeat
Of relentless change.

Reorientation

Do not seek me
In a computer screen,
Memo pad,
Or filing drawer.

I'll not be found
In impassioned speech,
High finance,
Or seminar rooms.

Nor am I defined
By shopping lists,
Car repairs,
Groaning meals,
Or TV plots.

Rather,
Find me in
The white gull's sweep;
In rippled sand;
In white crests
Of crashing surf;
And in strands of clouds
That blot the sun.

For these I'll leave
The world's clash and clamor—
Its mindless schedules
And obscene politics—
To those enamored
Of such things.

My soul's astride
The brown pelican
That in silent sweep
Glides above the roof,
Pressing toward eternity.

New Smyrna Beach

Here
We hold at bay
The clangs and clamors
Of obligation—
Bills to pay,
Doctors to consult,
Shrubbery to prune—
The bric-a-brac of daily life,
And instead embrace
One fragile interlude
Of heedlessness.

These days
Are hollowed out
For thought to evolve,
Expand,
Reflect,
Curl back upon itself,
And pour back
In deep conversation
At Happy Hour.

So, too,
One brisk walk along the beach
Is worth ten motor trips;
The quick snooze in afternoon
Trumps a night's restless slumber.
Art shows feed each sense,
And a restaurant meal
Offers new delights.

Cocooned in cozy settings—
The rolling sea our white noise—
We ignore the TV rantings
Of politicians
And appliance salesmen
As we build walls around our felicity,
Never (seldom) counting the hours
Until the world intrudes
Once more.

Watching for Pelicans

Barney Bear sits quietly
Atop his television perch
Gazing at the sky
Through sliding doors,
Watching for pelicans,
The deep-jawed birds
That ride the swirling winds
In groups of three or four
Above our condo roof.

At home in summertime
He spends his daylight hours
Peering solemnly
At flowers on the deck.
But winter in the South
Means pelicans to him.

Some days he spies
Small clusters gliding north
To whatever destiny awaits;
At other times
The sky is empty blue.

No matter.
Barney's hope is constant,
His eyes unglazed,
Patience unslacking,
Small body erect, relaxed.
And when he spots their graceful flight,
He's too much the gentleman
To make a sound,
But his eyes gleam
In sheer delight.

Meanwhile below:
Voices in the pool;
Clink of shuffleboard discs.
On the street
The endless swish of traffic.

Beyond,
Shoppers in the market;
Suffering people in Afghanistan;
UN debates;
Dog shows;
Garbage trucks;
Planes departing—
The jumbled cacophony of life
That soon rends the body
And numbs the brain.

Let it pass.
Take comfort.
Barney sits in tranquil hope,
Watching for pelicans.

When the Pelicans Come

Deep in conversation,
Wine glasses in hand,
We discourse learnedly
On revolutions,
Travel books,
Mideast potentates,
And health care plans.

But all talk ceases
When the pelicans come,

In ragged lines of three or more.
Gliding swiftly over our condo roof,
Exciting our little bear Barney—
And us, as well.

Strolling the flat expanse of beach,
We remark on the steady north wind,
Identify sea birds,
And chuckle at blimps
In taut bathing suits.
But as we scan the skies,

All diversions end
When the pelicans come.

We count their numbers,
Watch their flight
Over our distant building,
And rejoice that from his TV perch
Barney sees them, too,
His glass eyes gleaming
In ecstasy.

And on those days
When the air yields
Only the ever-circling gulls,
A noisy helicopter,
And a stray kite or two,
We give Barney an extra hug
At bedtime and promise him
(Fingers crossed)
That tomorrow
Will be another time
When the pelicans come.

Top Dog

Nine terns and a gull
Lounged on the beach
As I approached.

My footsteps raised heads
And ruffled feathers
But no one moved,

Until the gull,
Delicately lifting a skinny leg,
Waded determinedly
Into the surf,

To be followed
By his obedient harem.

Clouds and Sky

Clouds and sky
Mingle, interweave, diverge,
Forming patterns vivid enough
For an Impressionist's palette.

Through the passing days
We behold:

Blankets of low clouds
Slowly drifting,
With patches of sky
Breaking the solid covering;

Streaks of white clouds
Strung out across
The sky's blue expanse;

Wispy cloud strings floating off,
Leaving an azure blue sky—
Birdless, kiteless, featureless;

Small strips of white clouds
Marooned alone in a dominant sky;

Long strings of light grey clouds,
Fluffy white at their edges,
Giving way to pale blue sky;

Broken layers of pale grey clouds
Strung out in thick bands
Across a pallid sky;

Two narrow parallel lines of grey clouds
Dimly bisecting an empty sky.

Thus nature displays her myriad allures
Before our wondrous eyes.

In the Pool

Below in the courtyard
Father and son splash happily
In the pool's blue waters,

Father released at last
From tight neckties,
Unbreakable schedules,
Interminable meetings,
His mouth wide in a joyous whoop,

With son free to not
Comb his hair,
Sit up straight,
Be in bed by nine,
His exultant screech
Echoing off the condo walls.

For them
The cage of duty and decorum
Gaps open,
And together they abandon themselves
To play no less exuberant
For lasting
But a moment.

Heroes

Down from wintry Michigan
They came seeking Florida warmth.
He with wheeled walker,
Oxygen tank,
And thankful grin;
She with stooped back
And shining eyes.

They lolled in the heated pool,
Chatting with fellow bathers,
The tank squatting patiently
On tile's edge
For his return.

That night, a party,
And there they were,
Eating casserole and chocolate cake,
Talking with smiles,
The tank ever-present,
The walker waiting next to his chair.
In odd moments
She stroked him fondly.

Those who enter burning buildings
Are undoubted heroes;
And likewise soldiers defying sniper fire.
Nor should those who subsist
On beans and toast in run-down flats
Be forgotten.

Then surely travelers
Who live to live
Despite the odds,
Deserve such plaudits, too.

The Restaurant(s)

The Japanese restaurant
That stood in the mall
Is gone,
Its windows empty of the blinds
That shielded its décor,
A "To Let" sign taped on its pane.

We stepped last year
Onto checkered floors,
As in a barber shop,
And sat at a black lacquered table.
Hot tea and a warm towel
Soon appeared.
With chopsticks we ate
Bits of sushi dipped in sauce
From small bowls,
And drank the mild green tea.
We delighted.
Our server smiled.
We were happy.

This year we will miss
Our Japanese flavors,
But down the road
We discovered a restaurant
That serves Spanish dishes.

We are happy again.

Departure

Down the elevator
To the car
Go the bags,
Awakened now
After three months
Of peaceful slumber.

Behind,
The apartment
Morphs to empty space,
Its loneliness echoing
The leisured hours
It offered selflessly.

Implacable time
Creeps forward:
Our tomorrows
Have shrunk to yesterdays,
Become today,
And out,

And so our world
Swings north
To different scenes—
One stage complete,
Another to commence,
Like doors
Opening and shutting endlessly.

The Mail

Back from Florida:
Three months
Of sun, beaches,
And heedless hours.
Now the mail awaits—
Four boxes full.

Piles of
Enticements, invitations,
Admonitions, alarms,
And densely-paragraphed articles,
As the print world
Clamors for attention.

To wit:
"Look Inside! Free Gift!"
"Bonus Offer Enclosed!"
"Buy Two Sets and Save!"
"It's Time to Renew Your Subscription!"
"Do You have a Wheat Belly?"
"Our Retirement Security is at Risk!"
"The Worst Place to be when You're Sick."
"Cuba Hurtles toward Capitalism."
"The Best Summer in North America."

Fingers fly—
This bears reading;
That can be tossed.
The mind grows weary;
The rubbish bag fills.

Weeks pass.
The mounds shrink daily,
'Til at last one bright day
The boxes stand empty—
As we pack once more
For our Southern sojourn.

Hearth & Home

Anchors

Each day
I could get lost among the stars,
Whirling with them
Through vast realms
Of empty space,
My bones dissolving
In the silent reaches
Of the universe's eternal night;
My blood thinning down to vapor
And disappearing
In some stellar cloud
Swirling through endless time.

But,
Gazing out,
I spy the sturdy oak
Rooted in our front yard,
And exalt
In its leafy fullness.

Turning,
I see the morning sun
Slanting through the eastern windows,
Bathing me
In its mellow radiance.

Then through the hours,
I rehearse the composition
Of familiar scenes:
My loving wife's gentle smile;
Plants scattered about the house;
The town's narrow thoroughfares;
Our Teddy perched high atop
The sunroom love seat;
Majestic music from the CD;
The very rocks that dot our garden.

Each melds my spirit
Into infinite shapes,
As I seek meanings
Within the special moments
Of this place and time.

Thus, it is written:
The stars must wait.

Remembrance

If I tread village walks
Beneath dappled sunlight,

Or gaze at evening's darkening sky
From my bedroom window,

Or yet again construct mind-caverns
In which to ponder
Truth, beauty, God, and more,

Are such felicities but a whisper
Amidst life's pitiless clamor,
To vanish as mist upon a morning lake?

No,
For I shall cherish
These fleeting joys,
If not for eternity,
At least until tomorrow.

Night Thoughts

Give me
Silent streets;
Deserted parking lots;
The soft glow of lamps
Haloing silent pavements;
And dim bedroom lights
In darkened homes.

Night
Stills the day's mindless clatter;
Dissolves pain's knots;
Soothes the aching bones
That betray one's years.

In bed,
My head caressed
By one soft pillow;
My body enveloped
In warming blankets;
I banish the clamorous world
And—smiling—
Enter the vast universe
Of sleep.

Purification

Deep in the night
I awaken to the rumble
Of the furnace
Beneath our bedroom.

And feel at last
The day's long passage,
Swept clean now
Of groceries, politics,
And car repairs
That stop up the channels
Of quietude
And love.

Thus reassured,
I plump my pillow,
And fall back to sleep,
Held fast
In time's enduring embrace.

On Being Married Fifty Years

Deep in the moment,
Her eyes gleam
In the candlelight
Over the salmon pate
And next table chatter.
Glasses up.
To love.

Love threads down the years
Through morning coffee,
Breakfast tables,
Workday schedules
And home—
A union transcending
The pleasures of Happy Hour
While preserving
Each distinction.

If she adores skaters
And I cheer quarterbacks;
She shines at parties
While I'm silent at her elbow;
She walks carefully
While I stride out—
Yet her being reflects me
And mine hers,
Our oneness as vital as breathing,
Pervasive as air,
Deeper than feeling,

An affinity
Woven through two thousand days
As we dissect the world
And create our own realities:
The irrationalities of politics;
Planning a new bathroom;
A trip to Nantucket.

And when passion surges,
Love's touch presides
Through wit and laughter
As we explore each other's smoothness,
Climbing the heights.

Blessed by a love
Sanctified by five decades,
Perhaps we two as one—
Yet always two—
Cross thresholds
Of whatever divinity
This life permits.

Credit

I'd like to get eternal credit
(besides from my ever-grateful wife)
For performing all those little chores
An active household requires.

Maybe the Big Force upstairs
(Assuming it's there at all)
Maintains a ledger book It writes in when:
I clean the shower stall;
Run the dishwasher when its full;
Pay the bills on time.

Perhaps the Old Boy (or Girl)
Keeps a daily log of how often:
I put my dirty clothes in the hamper;
Take out the trash;
Weed the garden.

Very likely these days
It uses a computer to tally up:
How often I sweep the garage;
Dust the furniture;
Or buy the party wine.

Of course, such matters
Run in both directions;
I surely would get points deducted for:
Not putting my khaki pants in the wash;
Forgetting to return the milk carton
To the frig;
Being too slothful to sort out
My book collection;
Postponing getting the car tuned up.

Still, when the time comes
And I'm lined up in front of
The Pearly Gates, or whatever,
I think I'll have a pretty decent record
Of exemplary behavior.

Tile Worlds

Behold a tile bathroom floor,
Its squares laid end to end
And side to side.
From above,
Each patterns its own universe—
Varied strands of wavy nebulae
And swirling clouds
Stretching to the adjoining panel.

But draw close;
Peer down;
See what other images emerge
From each square's configurations.

In this square,
The thick, curved finger
Of sub-continent India;

Nearby,
A child with sunken face,
Mouth trailing down
Its right cheek;

Over there,
A mushroom cloud
Rising out of
Jagged, billowing whiteness;

Further on,
This square displays
A man's misshapen face,
With thick nose,
Mouth curved into a bow,
Eyes wide in awe or fear;

Next,
An Octopus with single evil eye,
Its lone, curling tendril
Snaking to the square's edge;

And then,
A scowling teddy bear
With black hole eyes
And faint, turned-down mouth;
Just above, a long-nosed sheep
Gazing placidly at the bear.

Who could know
What strange forms
The mind conjures
From the factory patterns
Of one tile floor!

Arborvitae Time

Bordering our back property end to end,
Thirty-four arborvitae stand,
Vigilant sentries blocking out
The thrusting thorn berries behind them
While finding shelter beneath
Three ancient ash trees.

Planted in the early '90s,
The evergreens bear witness
To time's remorseless passage.
They rise this day thinner
And more bowed,
Victims of the deer winter appetites;
The heavy snows of mid-season;
And March ice storms'
Deadly glistenings.

Yet there they are,
Still green and upright,
Rooted securely in pungent mulch;
Open to the summer winds and warmth;
Defying nature's continuing efforts
To bring them down.

Gazing upon these weathered trees
On a fine April day,
The sun smiling on their clustered needles,
What better model, I ask myself,
Could I seek
For my own life's journey?

God In The Flowers

Our deck radiates flowers.

Spreading out
From pots of many patterns
That rest on grey boards
Or rise from artful tripods,

The blossoms at midday glow
Red, white, purple, orange,
Velvet, pink, blue, yellow—
Shimmering fountains of color cascading
Across a sun-drenched platform,
And transforming its indifferent timbers
Into a layer
Of vibrant richness.

We gaze,
Awestruck at such deep beauty,
Convinced that
If divinity there be,
God is in the flowers.

Where The Weeds Grow

In the dark, damp places
The weeds grow.

Sheltered beneath
The Japanese maple
And Ornamental Grass,
Tiny clovers peep defiantly
From last year's mulch,
Prompting a resigned sigh,
Quick pluck,
And ever-filling basket.

Yet in brief life
These wee ones triumph,
Knowing that tomorrow's rain
Will spread their kin
Across the garden
Another time.

Kinky Hose

There are kinky ideas,
We know,
And kinky personalities,
As well,
Not to mention kinky sex.

And then there are kinky hoses.

You know,
The kind of hose
That curls and twists like a snake,
Halting the flow of water
Meant to relieve the garden plants
Wilting in the summer heat.

So you wrestle with the coil,
Pulling and tugging
Until at last the tangle
Curves flat,
Lying complacently on the grass.
You turn the water back on
And—naturally—the kink returns,

Yielding only to a second round
Of hand acrobatics
(Accompanied, this time, by curses)
Until your tormentor again stretches
Serenely across the yard.
Once more the water surges through—
And stops:
Two kinks, this time!

You scream to the heavens.
Kick the hose,
Shut off the water.
Go in to dinner.

Before bedtime
You'll sprinkle can
Those poor, parched plants,
And give that useless hose
Another kick.

Leaves

Shaken from their summer homes,
The colored leaves
Drift slowly onto our deck,
Scattering into narrow bands
That snake across its length.
Or clustering around the potted mums
That line the railings.

Remnants of the waning year,
They sprawl atop each other
Or hug the wood's smooth hardness,
Absorbing both the lingering warmth
And the gathering chill
Of autumn's hours.

Soon enough they will be broomed
Onto the lawn below,
There briefly to feel the damp grass
Before being swept away,
Like us,
To final oblivion.

Raw Days

While outside
The days turn raw,
In the sun room
Violets grow,
Nurtured by gentle hands
And fertilizer;
Caressed by the fire's warmth;
Their roots nestled securely
In moistened soil.

The white petals
Spread outward
Like velvet fingers embracing
The pale daylight,
And nod toward
The still-green grass
Stretching beyond
White-framed windows.

So do we all
Seek enrichments
That expand our constricted lives
In myriad ways,
As the days turn raw.

April Barren

Early April
This year
In Northern zones means
Dirty snow
In clumps and patches,
And rivulets of melt
Flowing swiftly
Through the ditches
Along the highways.

In backyards
The grass mats
Brown and wet,
The daffodils yet hidden
Beneath muddy soil.

Aloft,
Naked branches
Sway and whisper together
In obeisance
To a winter wind
That lingers late.
The air fills with
Swirls of grainy snow.

All is April barren
In these parts.
Poised,
Spring waits.

Teddy Bears

Our town boasts
A courthouse
With white pillars,
Attractive historic homes,
A sprawling Walmart's,
And dozens of teddy bears

Who emerge
On Festival Day in July,
To parade down main street
Amidst classic cars,
A fire engine,
Juggler,
Man on stilts,
Four-piece band,
And smiling marchers.

The bears
Lie in their small owners' arms;
Perch on grandpas' shoulders;
And crowd into roadster wagons
Pulled by moms and dads.
Color these little furries
Brown, blue, pink, green ,white,
And one jet black
(A special bear),
As they wave to onlookers
And the band plays "The Saints."

In the park
At the end of the route
The bears merge
Into the crowd
And soon head home,
To grace mantels,
Children's rooms,
And bed coverlets,
And dream
Of next year's big event.

Hydrant

Today in our town
They drained the fire hydrants,
Block by block,
Eventually reaching our lane.
They opened the nozzle with a wrench,
Releasing broad sheets of water
That arched across the road,
A controlled Tsunami
That soaked one lawn
And puddled the road
Before flowing harmlessly
Into the storm sewer.

Watching at the window,
We glimpsed the mysteries
Of nature's power,
Like witnessing a tiger in the zoo
Freed from his confines
By his handlers,
Then quickly re-ensnared.

And we shuddered
At what furies lay beyond
The fire plug's restraining cap
And the tiger's encircling bars.

The Jump

Introducing my horse,
Sir Thomas,
Mixed Thoroughbred-Appaloosa,
A trim gelding
With an easy gait,
Mischievous eye,
And cautious spirit.

For years
We trod forest paths,
Trotted down gentle slopes,
And cantered across grassy clearings,
And—most fun of all—
Leaped over painted jumps.

Approaching a jump,
My guy would hesitate.
Focusing my gaze,
I'd center him to the barrier,
Moving him into
A smooth, forward trot
Or rhythmic canter
By pressing my legs against his flanks,
Shifting my weight,
And adjusting the reins.
A trusting soul,
Sir T. would respond instantly
(Most of the time).

His pace, steady, even,
We moved closer ,
My body bent forward
And out of the saddle.
My head up.
The obstacle loomed.
Then up,
An instant airborne,
Horse and rider one.
Exhilaration!

To be followed by
A balanced landing
And flowing trot.
A moment's relief.
And the sheer sweetness
Of a successful jump.

On The Roof

He scrambles
Up the sturdy ladder
With practiced skill,
And like a colossus,
Bestrides the roof,
His boots thumping against the slope
As he searches for loosened tiles
That could drip rainwater
Onto innocent ceilings and support beams.

He scampers down
And proclaims to our anxious ears
That all is well:
The tiles aren't worn;
The nails still hold;
Both should withstand
Years of snowy winters.

Then, with a grin,
He is gone like superman,
Leaving us
In high relief,
A smoother day
To navigate—
And one more name to add
To our list of home repairmen.

Seasons' Strengths

Deftly he guides his mower
On its weekly journey
Across our lawn,
The blades set to spare
An exact three inches of green.
His green T-shirt clings tightly
To his muscular arms and chest,
His torso bare of sweater or jacket
On all but the coldest days.

In fall he mounts a ladder,
Moving it down our line of arborvitae
To erect a stout wire fence
Meant to thwart deer appetites
When the snows pile up.

Come spring, he uproots said fence,
Rolls it up,
And deposits it
Behind the evergreens,
Cradling the heavy wire in his arms
Like a plastic play toy.

Over his shoulder
He carries yards of hose
From their season's storage room,
Arousing, as he does so,
Our unbounded admiration;
Years past, my wife and I
Together strained to lift the hose
A scant inch or two
Above the ground.

In his wheelbarrow
He trundles heavy piles of mulch
To waiting flower beds,
And with his shovel
Skillfully spreads the rich soil
Around the tiny plants.

Never daunted,
He flashes a ready grin
That reflects his rugged geniality
As he pursues his numerous tasks.
Slow-bodied and ripe with years,
We cherish his cheerful prowess
And the satisfactions
His yearly exertions provide.

Barney

You came to us in time of trial:
A little bear with black glossy fur,
Two round glass eyes,
A dimpled nose,
And one bent strip of down-turned mouth—
And oh so quickly
Stole our hearts.

By day you sit in dignified repose
Atop a loveseat sofa back,
And gaze through sliding doors
At flowers clustered on the deck
(What secrets do the petals tell
When we are not at home?
What tales do you recite to them?)

As evening falls, you cuddle in our laps
At Happy Hour and crossword puzzle time,
Helping Jim fill in the lettered squares.
And later, nestle peacefully
As we read, or surf the tube.

Little bear, so silent;
What mysteries might you unveil,
What scenes illuminate,
Could you give voice to private dreams?

Little bear
So powerless. and yet
So powerful.

25079133R00102

Made in the USA
Middletown, DE
16 October 2015